Table of Content

- Suicide Notes
- Denial
- Bargaining
- Anger
- Depression
- Acceptance
- Love Life

Preface

Who are The Lost Poets? We are a poetic group of worldwide writers who are coming together to shine a light on topics that affect humanity on a wide scale. As a collective, we acknowledge controversial topics, in high hopes of enlightening others.

LET'S DROP THE SUICIDE RATE. FIGHT WITH US. We cannot do this without YOU!

"I think the society is sick, not us. Take the same people and put them in a different setting and they'll thrive"-B.F., California, RN

"I think that there are two different views. On one side an increase of mental health issues could mean that more people seek help and get diagnosed so that's a positive development. On the other side, there is a lot of pressure on children today, most countries school systems really suck, and I think that is really is a big concern. I also think it's problematic that we try to just treat everything with antidepressants without even trying to find out the underlying causes of mental illness. They're just trying to tell us to take a couple of pills and go back to work. In my opinion, that's not the kind of therapy that's needed and it won't solve the actual issues in many cases." – A.K., B.A. Psychology

"I have a lot to say about mental health. In summary, it's all within each person to change their own mindset. Only as individuals do we each have that power. The miracle to heal the mind, body, soul lies within."K.D., Bachelor of Health Science and Biology

Suicide Notes

Daisy Bojorquez - Biography

Daisy Bojorquez is an artist and poet living in Southern California with her husband and fur baby Oreo. Despite having a mental illness and a difficult life with the help from God and her great support system she was able to survive and she became a loving, sensitive and emphatic person. Happily married to her wonderful loving husband that has been a huge comfort and help during rough times and full of laughter, silliness, and smiles during the good times. Since a young age, she has had a true passion for the arts. Every chance Daisy had she immersed herself in her artwork and her poetry. Her art was a sort of therapy that was one of the things that helped her to survive. She studied at El Camino College where she obtained her Associate in Arts degree with a major in Art. When Daisy first heard about this poetry project her heart opened and she couldn't wait to start writing. She wanted to comfort and help others going through difficult times. Her goal was to at least help someone in need and to help them hang on one more day. Her heart goes out to those in need. Daisy states that she wants to dedicate this to her wonderful husband and her best friend. She couldn't have made it without them in her life.

Daisy's Suicide Note

Finally.

I just wanted the pain to stop.

But...

Did I really just do this?

Oh my God...

Wait...

My life is passing by my eyes.

I see my parent's faces.

I see my best friend's face.

I see the face of my love.

Wait...

Now I see them crying.

Sobbing.

I see them blaming themselves.

All of a sudden I don't know if I want this...

This was supposed to be release for me...for them...

I thought I was just a heavy burden...

No one completely understood.

The pain and the sadness that engulfed me each day...

But they still loved me.

My life continues to leave me...

Oh my God I was wrong...

What did I............

Daisy Bojorquez

EBUKUN GBEMISOLA OGUNYEMI (IBUKUNWRITES)- Biography

Ebukun Gbemisola Ogunyemi better known as Ibukunwrites is a Nigerian Poet, Storyteller and Creative Writer born as Ogunyemi Blessing Gbemisola. Her works are inspired by so many things around her from little conversations to nature, experiences (both personal and non-personal) and more. As a survivor of trauma, Ibukunwrites is very passionate about women, children, family, parenting, abuse, mental health, and emotional related causes; most of which she tries bringing to life in her writings without holding back. She's very simple, witty, resilient and big on documentaries and she hopes to have her own talk show one day. Ibukunwrites writes to shed light, bring light, hope, and restoration.

She blogs at http://www.ibukunwrites.com and she can be found on social media through these links:

Facebook – https://www.facebook.com/ibukunwrites/

Instagram – https://www.instagram.com/ibukunwrites/

Twitter – https://twitter.com/ibukunwrites/

Ebukun's Suicide Note

This is the suicide note
I never wrote on days when I
tried taking my own life but chickened out.
This is the exhaustion I couldn't put into words
because I had absolutely nothing to pour
too stressed to write
I just wanted to leave
No one wants you when you're here but
everyone suddenly wants you to stay when you're gone
I told myself
I had no loved one to write to
Whatever they made of my demise, I could care less
but I guess I was mad
I was mad about the love I constantly sought but
never got.
but isn't this life
Isn't my life worth more than a protest?
Isn't this life given to me for a reason?
Isn't this life mine and no one else's for a reason?
Yes, I thought as much.
The reason I have to fight this hard is because
I have the ability to survive
so today and every other day, I'll choose to stay
this space is mine, this space belongs to me
so I just don't get to walk away
so today and every other day
I'll choose to stay, I'll choose to fight
I'll resist the urge to die and fight one last time
until there are no wars - no wars to be fought.

Ibukunwrites

Sabrina Eden -Biography

Given the name Sabrina Jomichelle Mouton, this American writer, photographer and artist is ready to take on any obstacle. Not only has she struggled with mental illness, but she has conquered twenty years of abuse, neglect and trauma. Sabrina has lost loved ones to suicide and attempted suicide as a teen. As an independent adult, she has adopted the name Sabrina "Eerie" Eden and is dedicating her life to the arts in hopes of ridding the world of its corruption. She hopes to inspire others to live. Mental illness not only having affected her but also some very dear to her. "To my sassy, hilarious and beautiful nieces, Jasmine and Meadow, fight your demons. You are a reason I write and one of the reasons I fight my demons too."

Sabrina openly states "I am more than honored to be a part of this project. I want someone to pick up this book and ponder one of two things. Either 'Woah, someone understands me.' or 'Wow. Maybe I should be more considerate of other's emotional and mental wellbeing."

Sabrina's Suicide Note

I will not fight nature, anymore

Everyone, agrees that I'm a whore

There's nothing left worth living for

My pride, my life has been torn

There's nothing left but a shell

My heart, heavy and in mourn

This life since birth has been hell

No one loves me, even my own mother left me for dead

All the missed days "Happy Birthday" she never said

No one loves me even my own blood neglects and rapes me in the end I am afraid of the events in the path ahead

Everyone treats me like shit

Perhaps it's because I am full of it

My body is a punching bag for fists

My thighs are gashed with slits

My parents hate me

My friends shame me

My lovers won't date me

There's no one left to blame, except me

I've put down my battle sword of words overexerted from being a burden nothing is worth this

I am drowning in the deepest depths of dread I would rather physically drown instead

I am teary and emotional

Peering at the crystal water in the Jacuzzi

I am going through with this I am beginning to feel woozy

The time has come to do it

"If I make it out alive it's not by my own means

If I make it out alive give me something to hold onto something to believe

No one loves me

So I here I go

Into the shallow depths

May death come slow

Reaper, take my grief

Make me hollow"

Can you hear me, euphoria?

Because I can feel you

A current that drifts around me

A relief from dystopia

What they never

Tell you about drowning

Is that floating down feels so accommodating?

Out of this realm

Out of my element

Take me away

Take me away I can't see I can't breathe

But I can feel you

Lifting me high

Onto cloud nine

Floating Weightless

Floating Weightless

Sabrina Eden

Spencer Ross- Biography

Spencer Ross, born and raised in Madison, Wisconsin. I'm the 5th child out of seven siblings. Raised in a nice neighborhood and school system of Madison. Began Writing poetry a few months ago out of curiosity. Throw my work on Instagram and Vince asked if I wanted to help with this book. My pen name is Intellectual difference. One, because everyone is intellectual in their way. But it also represents Unity between us. Being human beings on this gravitating rock flying through space. We all feel its pain but we can't always explain why this is. I never got any help for my depression. I thought I didn't need any. Thought I could conquer this thing in my head. It's more than that. It's this thing that breaks you down. Slowly crushing your spirit so much that eventually, you can't take it. It will break you. It broke me. Poetry and music have been my fall back addictions. Slowly bringing me back from this long overdue rut. Stuck in the mud. Life flying by three years at a time. When will this bad trip end? When I am actually dead. But I am not ready for that. I got too much potential in my head. I can't give up now, I'm too far in. Let me write another line before I sin again.

Spencer's Suicide Note

At a very young age I felt alone,

Scared of what others thought,

Fearful,

my mind thrived there,

becoming what it is today,

depression upgraded me,

why would I cry when I can laugh hysterically at the pain driving me,

wishing I could just give up,

but that would be a shortcut,

I am too far to just wipe clean,

Death will come don't rush it,

Your life was given to you out of love,

Don't give it up because the demons scold you,

Fight back,

Show that you have had enough of their games,

I know I have,

Depression has got the best if me,

I trudge through the storm,

Hopefully to see another day,

Hopefully helping a few more people along the way,

Stuck screaming in the dark,

Hold on I will bring the light that way

Intellectual Difference

Vincent Osborne- Biography

My name is Vincent J Osborne I'm from Long Beach CA. I grew up living through drive by shootings and school riots. Most of my life I was poor and even though my family was large, in many ways I felt like an orphan. At 14 I went through multiple traumatic experiences that caused me to start considering suicide. At 25 I was committed to a mental institution and was diagnosed with psychotic disorder and social anxiety. For the next 3 years I was in a medicated haze and I had tried everything from religion to meditation. I was at an all time low. I wrote my Suicide Note and walked to the side of a highway and sat in the snow and waited to freeze to death. After about 20 minutes I decided it wasn't cold enough to freeze as quickly as I needed and I decided to try it again the next day. I went home and came to a realization that I could do good still and the world needed help. I began eating healthy and practicing self love. I began to feel better, stronger, more focused. I was able to stop taking my medication and stop smoking. I knew I needed to do what I could to bring light to the fact that people are hurting and making drastic decisions they can't take back. Please read this book with an open mind and if you know someone who could benefit from the heartfelt poetry and mantras in this book please give them a copy. @vincethapoet all platforms.

Vincent's Suicide Note

A wondering soul

Simply warmer than most

Wondered if today were his "last"

How long would it go on?

Is "last" finale or infinite?

If words depend on contexts

Do the seasons offer sentiment?

Him reasoning this, winter leaves the trees so thin

But in the spring the birds sing, who taught them how to sing like that?

And if birds sing do songs ever really end?

Thus he sit wondering is "last" finale or infinite.

Was he man of men or a seed that took root and grew into a candle wick?

Though his flame flickered could the wind dismantle it?

Like the smoke that remains, leaving the room scented with its presence.

He wondered, is "last" finale or infinite?

When he bleeds his blood flows, it flows much like the river.

He may evaporate in the summer and freeze in December.

But his waves flow endlessly aligned. So how could "last" be based on time

When time is infinite?

If the world should end has it ended endlessly?

With lips he spoke, his heart did beat, but his soul had lived beyond what time had seen.

Do the clouds encompass us the way that we encompass meat?

If the world should end today, he reasoned, I'll start another dream.

Vincent J Osborne

Denial

Compulsion (OCD)

I have to do it

For if I don't

There will be consequences

But if I do

A life may be lost

Mental fences

Intrusive, violent thoughts

Torturing, whiplashing my mind

I have to do it

For if I don't

There will be consequences

But if I do

Sanity may get lost

Heightened senses

Allusive, dangerous thoughts

Fracturing, attacking my mind

It makes me sick

These senseless crimes

I'm not sure what I am to do

About my repetitive compulsions

I am more than addicted

Without the high

I'm not sure what I am to do

I have to do it

For if I don't

There will be consequences

But if I do

The world may end

Doubting, like slipknots

Around the logic, throbbing my mind

It makes me tick

Will I ever defy

This chaos that leaves me out of order

Obsessive Compulsive Disorder

Sabrina Eden

Hideout

Hidden in this conscious,
trying to express that I don't like it,
only to be misspoken,
keeping my spirit intact,
not caring about the light snacks,
trying to eat the whole tab,
I ain't got time to throw my feelings in the trash,
so I back up and admire my work,
letting the feeling marinate in my self worth,
slowly getting comfortable with the lines I write,
instead of hiding away,
out of mind and sight.

Intellectual Difference

Dying Is Cheap

I'm a server at run down diner

My financial needs have grown tighter

In this stuffy building, I can hardly breathe

Groups of hungry people is all I see

They impatiently await their food

As I pour a cup of dark roast I hear "Hey you!"

I look around and no one is looking my way

So I turn away

but I hear it over and over

the voices are taking over

someone won't stop calling my name

I can't focus, it's driving me insane

So I look around the restaurant once more

I am confused

This caffeine addicted customer looks unamused

I am sidetracked

By auditory hallucinations

I want to cry when I realize that

In my body,

there comes a depressed sensation

I lift the cup of coffee and proceed to give to them

Even though I try to continue to do my job

Customers still get mad at me when I ignore them

I wish I could tell them that they were wrong

They do not realize how difficult it is to tell the difference

Between what is real and what is in my head

The voices are so rigorous

On my reality they continue to breed

Until all the customers leave

By then my tips are a mere two-twenty three

When living is an expense,

"Dying is cheap"

becomes a relieving belief

Sabrina Eden

Half of Us

Half of this youth carries it

But we don't reveal

Our inner truth

In fear of misconception

Half of us feel unusual

Yet we continue to conceal

Our inner truth

In fear of rejection

Half of us are drowning in our demons

Can we fight what we feel?

Our inner truths

Without fearing other's perceptions

We are more

Than this half of us

We are more

Than our mental illness

Sabrina Eden

Home

There is no place
like home.
I like to think
it depends on where you call home.
Home is where joy is inconsistent.

Home is a place I cannot
wait to leave.
Home is a thorn in my
flesh.
Home is nothing but a trigger;
a place where what dies
constantly and needlessly survives.
Home is a place I run from.
Home is where I find sadness
without a longing.
Home is a place
I'd rather not be.

Ibukunwrites

I hate hospitals

I hate hospitals.

Not because the people stare.

Not because the nurse was rude.

Not because of the uncomfortable chairs.

Not because because they smell like poop.

Not because the food is bad.

Not because they tell the truth.

Not because the people are sad.

Not because the doctors make loot.

Not because of the bums outside.

Not because of the paper work.

Not because the medication they prescribed.

Not because I don't think they work.

I hate hospitals because they tell me to do something I never do…

Think of ME first.

Vincent J Osborne

Just One More Drink

I wanted an escape.

I wanted to keep drinking.

I never want to stop.

Anything but this sad life I lead.

Hide it all behind a smile.

Till I can drink and drink some more.

I say out loud that I deserve it after having such a terrible day... such a difficult life...

No one knows the truth why I act so fun and crazy.

I'm desperate to hide what I really feel.

So I just say I deserve it while others laugh, drink and cheer.

It numbs me and slows me down until I get sick from the overwhelming amount I just drank.

I don't want to go back to reality.

It hurts too much.

People just don't understand.

Daisy Bojorquez

Life

Life is good, life is great, going through these bars like I'm a saint,

ready for more but told I can't take it,

kicked out of the club cause I am too great man,

thrown from the building

Not really knowing why,

didn't want to learn a useless trade,

like the people next to me, wanted to be something more,

something amazing that everyone could be,

so at a young age started spitting the truth to all who lied and hated,

showing the way to the ones that were hurting,

ready for more but I can't take cause i'm still a saint,

ready for the silence to end,

so I build up an army of 12 friends and try to teach the good we can unleash,

I show my real conscious to all who want to see,

showing how powerful I could be just by being me,

I climb up the stairs just to be pushed away again,

I'm in control but I can't take it, try to end it but I ain't ready for the storm to end,

the storm of life is the storm of all, capturing all, using all, remaking, carnating, all that dies to form new life, I was that new life,

why would I cut my time when all I got is time,

life seasons affect all even the guy in the sky,

stop trying to change in a way that doesn't feel right,

listen to the voices in your head, they make the most sense,

maybe showing you how cruel things real get,

maybe changing our destiny is the ultimate demise,

death is a start in the right direction, maybe in the opposite,

I don't got time to comprehend it, life is short enough,

don't be someone you aren't, be bold, stand out,

show all who really has the power,

make them shake and tremble and maybe they will throw you off too,

but only time will tell, if you make it in a book of lies,

making people get captivated by another god of time.

Intellectual Difference

Fallacious Love, Confusion

Being mentally ill brings upon confusion

Making us easier targets for abuse

We can get so carried away

that our sense of self diffuses

He held me by a noose

I was lead to believe

that he was the boy of my dreams

love was far from reality

It was tough

Being in lust

with him and his schemes

He hit me rough

It was extreme

Fallacious was this love

If I could go back in time

and tell myself one thing

I would tell myself to stop the grieving

"He doesn't love you, you need to leave

Don't let anybody make you believe

That love comes in a form of violence

Take your heart and guide it

For there is someone out there

who will take your love and redefine it"

Sabrina Eden

Monday Madness

I have to keep my wit

I can't be too quick to admit

If they'd like to make a trade it's gon' have to be legit.

I see they really want my soul

They don't know it's made of gold.

I think I'ma live forever.

They say I'm crazy as a crow.

Medication didn't help.

I'm the chair that wouldn't fold.

I keep burning from within,

I'm somewhat like a wooden stove.

They keep giving in to sin,

I gave in and couldn't cope.

I get high and see the truth,

Then they say I shouldn't smoke.

Vincent J Osborne

Nothing To Atone

A lovely woman just lost the love of her life

Sobbing, bending over the casket

I don't know how to comfort her

Even though she is a mess

I long to relate

I am so numb

She hates me for it

Called me cruel

I don't feel evil

I feel nothing

Nothing at all

I wish I could get a clue

On what it's like to feel blue

Life goes on,

Don't you know?

I wish I knew what it meant to be whole

So I could comfort her

In all honesty,

I have nothing to atone

Sabrina Eden

Productive Physique

They smile and wave
They say hello and goodbye
They acknowledge me
But not my internal disease

I wonder what they would say
If I showed them the things that live inside
Beyond my skin, the real me
My wicked self, my internal physique

Would they run in fear of what they do not know?
Would they hold me close and never let me go?
Who's to say
Who's to know

How others would react
If we saw each others monsters
Could we still acknowledge the fact
That our hearts can still be fostered

Sabrina Eden

Queen of Misery

In the aftermath

My skin is coated in resin

Much like the reason

The smoke has dissipated

I am a constant rainy season

Blackened tears are the acid rain

Self treason

burning my cheeks

Hoarding on the ground

Boom goes my lightening tongue

simultaneous is the sound

of false pretenses

Tragedy is bound

To strike again

Queen of Misery, I am crowned

As I walk through the puddles

my ancestors have left

Here I live awaiting death

Sabrina Eden

Selfish mind

Locking the door,
so none may enter,
hiding away so none will bother,
selfish thought linger over,
what once was the mind of a poet,
is the mind of a monster,
depression holding me under,
only taking breaths when I need it most,
embracing my poems instead of other addictions,
slowly showing my true potential through my art,
living a lonely life, and that's fine by me.

Intellectual Difference

These Voices in My Head

There are so many voices in my head
sometimes, I often get lost in them
There are many voices in my head
they don't stop when I want them to
they haunt
they torment
they poke
sometimes they get too loud
stronger
fiercer
meaner
exerting
controlling
these voices in my head
they encroach my space
they come crawling into my peace with chaos
these many voices – I hear them all
all except mine
but I want to hear mine
I want some decorum
still, this one thing I am;
a woman with many voices
finding clarity, creating boundaries and claiming territories.

Ibukunwrites

Video games

High school came and went but I didn't,

stuck in an endless game,

formed on hate and more hate,

living a life in a game far from the one that I was meant to be,

striking fear with ones online instead of the real ones in my life,

always going for one more level, shader or raid,

stuck in a vortex of grey, not knowing what was wrong with my life,

told that I needed to stop my addiction,

what addiction I asked myself, I am not doing drugs just playing a game,

 although I was terribly wrong,

everyday I got sucked in more and more, consuming more of my time like air,

revolving my life on a console,

instead of my loved ones who really cared,

held hostage by a posse of online lobbyists who only wanted my help not my connections, one day I broke down, knowing when I was going to stop playing,

stopped slaying, grabbed the consoles reins and threw them down the drain,

saw that my life was going to mush,

knowing that if I stopped now, I would have some luck

getting back to my social cage, where I am fed and slaved away,

life is life and we can't stop it from happening,

we can only work for our masters, so hopefully we can be a part of the bigger picture, maybe we can ever be someone's master one day,

or just slave away for all of our days.

Intellectual Difference

What if?

What if I'm in my own way?

What if I need to listen?

What if I'm not as good as I could be?

What if I'm a snowman?

What if I'm in my own way?

What if I should listen?

What if I'm not as good as I could be?

What if I should listen sooner?

What if I needed to grow up sooner?

What if I'm in my own way?

What if I'm not as good as I could be?

What if I should listen?

What if I needed to grow up?

Vincent J Osborne

Bargaining

Blues

The genre I write is the same one that helps me sleep at night,

fighting a war in my mind, I will surely lose with time, just holding the tide, don't break a sweat, before the midday blues,

I might lose a bet,

follow your heart if it leads to regret,

showing shit but never caving in,

wiping clean to smudge again,

life has choices and consequences,

leaving you dead one day was just the point of it,

leaving us hope was the worst of it,

leave us now before we riot.

Intellectual Difference

Darkness and Light

Complete utter darkness

Complete utter despair

Why did you bring me here?

How could you bring me here?

Why did you trigger me?

I did not want to feel this again

I'd rather feel the high

The power

The strength

The sparkling light

But yet I'm trapped

I am devastated each time it happens

Doomed to repeat and fall again.

And again.

And again.

There's a sickness that rocks me to my very core.

I rise but yet again I fall

Deeply into my melancholy

Deeper still

Until I can not breathe anymore

Where I don't want to breathe anymore

It's scary and beautiful at the same time

It's too deep

I fear I may drown

Deeper and deeper I fall

Just because I'm here doesn't mean I'm ok

Just because I'm here doesn't mean I want to be ok

Sometimes I just want to stop

Everything

Everything

Everything

Daisy Bojorquez

Fallen Angel

Angel...Angel...

Why do you cry...? Why do you cry...?

Angel...Angel...

Why do you feel so alone...?

Why do you not let me heal the aching of your heart...?

I am your angel and you are mine.

I see you...

I feel you...

Can you not see me...?

Can you not feel me...?

I am here...

I am here...

You don't have to feel alone.

But you pushed me away...

Where did you go that I could not follow?

My heart did not listen...could not listen.

Until this day.

Awakened from dreams of your former self...

Crashing into reality.

I became aware that my heart had been blinded by illusions and by castles in the sky.

It made my body so cold no fire ever could warm me.

One more thing I have to survive...

Again...

But yet... my heart beats...

Inhale...

Exhale...

Still alive.

My wings carry me out of this hole I had dug for myself and into the stillness of the night.

You had shed your angelic wings and have turned into a monster of

broken promises of friendship and of love.

You kept me from myself...

I suffered so much for you and you always seemed to bring me to my knees.

I could cause you no harm.

I loved you.

You did not listen to the whispers of my heart...

I longed to sing to you of my dreams.

"Perfection" wasted.

Now my heart is stronger.

With the raging that is inside this soul I will protect myself from you.

I am not your angel.

You are not my angel.

Daisy Bojorquez

Let there be light

Some days,
I think about dying.
other days,
I think about living.
most days,
I think about living before dying.
other times,
I wrestle against acute exhaustion.
and many times,
I think about seeing God.
but every day,
I look in the mirror and whisper to myself
"breathe, warrior!"
and in a flash,
I think about how forever
sometimes is less than time but
equal to moments.
and every night,
when I put myself to bed
amidst darkness and creeping fear
trying to displace my confidence eyes shut
haunted memories trying to play catch up with
the new realities I'm building
I gasp for breath
one finger down my throat
I'm vomiting fear & decreeing let there be light.

Ibukunwrites

Love of My Life

Before I met you there was point in my life where I truly hated myself.

I was very self destructive.

Not even caring anymore.

I thought no one cared if I lived or died.

I felt I was just an unbearable burden.

So why care?

Then I met you.

Such a beautiful soul inside and out.

You taught me to believe in love again.

This love is the kind that most people spend their whole lives dying and searching for.

This is the love we have together.

I can't believe at one point I almost lost you completely my love.

Destroying us with crazed thinking and actions.

I'm sorry.

Please keep loving me.

Please don't ever leave me.

Despite my limitations and my weaknesses you saw something inside of me that was still good and loving despite being full of darkness and pain.

You have saved me from the ugliness inside of myself countless times.

You are still here loving me unconditionally.

Your love has changed me forever.

All I can do is continue to love you.

Please don't give up on me my love.

Daisy Bojorquez

Making a Home Again

There are days I drown
days I'm nothing more than a soul roaming through
the emptiness of the streets
scouting for a home
and sitting close to the shore
after close of each day
finding none.
There are days I get tired of this routine
days I command the waters afraid
saying
bring my body back to me
and let my soul be at peace in a body once broken
for this body is mine
for this body is home
for this home I do not trade.
and this home, I'll always choose.

Ibukunwrites

May There Come A Day

Mother tells me I am a son of God
So I can never feel the way I do
She treats me like I am a fraud
As if my feeling aren't true

When she catches me cry
She says
"Enough! You are perfect,
my son of God."
In the presence of people,
I must constantly act alright
Otherwise,
I remember my mother yelling
saying that I am wrong

I put on a face of sarcasm everyday
To hide the terrible state of mind that lingers inside
No matter where I go or what I do,
I always feel this way
No matter who tells me what,
whatever they deny

At the end of each day
I dream away
Screaming, I say

"This is me!

You can't read my mind

For if you did maybe you could coincide

Instead of making me lie!"

May there come a day

When we can openly say

"I'm not okay"

By then,

it maybe three words

too late

Sabrina Eden

Maybe

I wish love is as sweet as its promises.
I wish it stays same and only gets better with age like a fine wine.
I wish love is always true.
maybe it is. maybe it's not. maybe it's just me.
maybe I'm just tired of letting love make a foolish woman out of me.
I know
I'm aware
that these songs of love are sweet
but these lovers are never as sweet as their words.
maybe it's just me. maybe I'm just paranoid. maybe I can't outlive my past experiences.
maybe you're right. maybe you're wrong.
maybe it's just something way too bigger for you to see.

Ibukunwrites

One minute

I gave you my minute and you gave me yours,
slowly falling in line,
not ready to realize the time we spent,
just want to keep the memories of what's left,
Time's presence still hanging over our heads,
death slowly creeping, times slowly drifting,
to a day when we will be separated for eternity,
so why not be together before that,
why waste the only time we have left,
don't let the clock suck you in.

Intellectual Difference

Overboard

I am a sailor on waves of pain

Losing consciences on failed escape

Worlds lost in overthought

A strive to become what I am not

Matter destroyed and redefined

Clustered gems of gold were mined

Only barren rock remains

No one but myself to blame

But pressure is still a constant strength

Confined to work in fallen grace

Pressing stone beyond repair

A desolate diamond with blinding glare

A sailor docking

Cold and weak

But struggle gave his life a face

Intellectual Difference

Panic

I just found out a horrible truth.

I can't escape it

It follows me around wherever I go

I used to think the terror would happen in a closed dark room.

In a tiny space.

I never thought I would feel it in an open meadow.

I thought I would be safe.

I'm not safe from it.

It begins with an overwhelming anxiety.

I have to go.

I have to get out.

I have to get away.

But what do I do when I'm already in an open place?

All the deep breathing means nothing right now.

I can barely breathe in and out.

I can't get enough air.

All I can do is feel it.

The tightness in my chest makes me feel like I am going to die.

I feel an intense heat in my chest that radiates to the rest of my body.

My brain can only focus on my heart beating erratically.

Why is everything spinning?

Oh God I feel like I'm going to be sick.

I feel strange sensations in my finger tips.

I'm overwhelmed with fear.

I need to get away.

Where do I need to go to get rid of these feelings?

I'm already out in the open.

Where do I go from here?

Finally everything seems to subside.

It takes so much out of me in every single way it can.

I can't do this anymore.

Daisy Bojorquez

The Star vs the night

She could freeze a room.

Uniquely cool.

Her swag could move and deepen moods.

One thing is true.

She always knew,

but greatness lead her to freedom.

Love's lessons learned her blessings.

Wanted but didn't need him,

or maybe she did but couldn't wait.

Can't bet on a loss it isn't safe.

Broken promises are out of date.

Where is he?

Will he come back?

And if he does is he ready?

He saw the look in her eyes...

It made him want to cure her doubts and heal her pain.

He knew he needed to take the oath.

She needed to SEE she came second only to God.

He was equally as happy to be in her presence.

Vincent J Osborne

The Decision

I'm on border's edge,

A crest of congested thoughts.

Wondering why a winner's prizes dwindles because at times he's lost

Counting cost like exchanged chains for change.

Only to see that debt freedom is the freedom to be captured

Like open game in this open game I'm destine to be caught

So commonly I'd seek the recipe to escape the fate that sought after me

Instead I found a road with no end one paved with regrets and no dividends.

Divided I sat...go hard? Or give in?

I'd rather risk my life to live my life then risk wasting my life being afraid to the end.

Vincent J Osborne

Why Me?

Anger is bubbling up inside of me.

A raging torrent fills me to my very core.

Why me?

Why me?

Why did I have to turn up like this?

Like something irreversibly defective.

My brain doesn't work like it should.

What evil have I committed to deserve this?

I know my thinking is wrong

Ha! What an understatement!

Sometimes I'm just filled with rage

Didn't I go through enough?

I've experienced bone crushing pain since I was a little girl

I hate sounding like a victim

A victim is usually considered weak

I am anything but weak to have survived this mental illness

that has affected of me in more ways than one.

Until my dreams of a perfect paradise come true I'm stuck with this.

I'm stuck with you.

Daisy Bojorquez

Anger

Apocalyptic World In My Eyes

The letters and numbers
on this page are spinning miles an hour
I can't wrap my head around
How everyone can work
As my vision blurs and I've silently gone berserk
Can't they hear my pleas and muffled screams
Can't they see my lost hope and dying dreams
Tearing me apart from the inside
How can everybody else function
Can't they see the destruction
Behind this wasted time
Behind authorities alibi
The clock is ticking
My reality in this moment is shrinking
My existence in this crowded class feels like a crime
How is everyone else doing just fine
Will they ever see the apocalyptic world in my eyes
Will they ever see my suffering even if I don't cry

Sabrina Eden

Feed the beast

Find the pain create the beast,
I don't want to look back at the pain just feed the beast.
Water food sleep feed the beast. Release it fear it be it,
I will work for eternity 1, be the beast,

Only you can see it and only you can free it,
Self control is not what I need, Scriptures say it will conquer you,
stay true stay in tune, I want to be free from the pain,
bring the dark in your everyday life to recreate the beast to other saints,
who don't have the pain inside to release their true destiny.

Intellectual Difference

Burning Rage or Cold Blood

You're an apple, No.

You're a dog, No.

You're a boy, No.

You're a hog, No.

You're a lizard, No.

You're a snake, No.

You're a witch, No.

You're a great, No.

You're a fire, No.

You're a snowman, No.

I snapped the coward's neck using both hands.

As he lay there dead we started to slow dance.

We watched his soul spill out like his chest was open.

I used to love but now I'm frozen.

She used to feel but now she's hopelessly.

A perfect pair made in hell.

Where this will go time will tell.

It's amazing when I blink.

It's the only time I see.

They say I'm dumb,

Or even slow

But they don't know

I'm just Cold Blooded.

Vincent J Osborne

Despise Me

Ignite me with your doubt

Wisdom will come about

From all my endeavors

Because I know that I am better

Because I am no settler

A clever mind will always fight the odds

A clever mind will always fight the wrong

When I pull on the last apple from the tree

How rewarding it will be

To see you lie to me

Tell me that you love me

With no apparent reason why

All you ever did was undermined me

I've already said goodbye

Despise me

Sabrina Eden

Fool In Recluse

You think it won't happen to you

Until it does

Then what

To tell or not to tell

What would speaking do

Would it erase the memories

Would I be shamed and ridiculed

I feel like a fool in recluse

My explicit imagery

I can't contain

I was used like a tool

Things will never be the same

I'm dirty and worn

Suffering in his frozen winds

leaving my sanity to rot

without any empathy

without a second thought

Sabrina Eden

Give up, I dare you

I gave up, I lost touch, am I wrong for that or did I toughen up,

I brought down the sun, holding firmly,

till the moon took its place, endless nights let my demons run wild,

wreaking havoc cross all platforms,

bringing down governments and rebellions,

destroying farms and reasonable notions,

for my time has finally risen to become the beast that I couldn't envision,

crawling further into disillusion, lord close my rendition,

for laughter has brought out my pain,

singing loudly in the streets, for all listening, I gave way, I entered the cosmos, I feel sane, it was pure joy, do it jump my way,

I may just drop you, but that's the change you will have to take,

come child of god bring your light this way.

Intellectual Difference

Gleam

The wanting in your eyes leads to more than you can fathom,

brain formed to seek out the horrors of tomorrow,

always leaning closer to death instead of leaning back enjoying what's left,

the world as we know it will be gone in an instant,

when we forget why we live on it,

not for money or power but for leaning on each other when we have no one else to bother,

Harmony's laughter will bring the world closer,

when people get out of their self worth,

getting offended at everyone cause you weren't okay with their self worth,

wanting more out of nothing and undoing what the world has made,

everything is okay and dandy in this rock floating in space,

far from our creators,

but not far enough from their pain.

Intellectual Difference

I've Always Been a Strong Woman

my defiance is not a product of how much you abused me.
it is delusional to think I became strong because you broke me
there is no good in your bad
you didn't build my strength
I did
I didn't need to be broken by you
to be called strong.
Surviving you was not a proof of my womanhood & strength
don't try to be
strength came with my womanhood
she's female
she's who I am
so
take my survival out of your mouth
true that
I was poised never to rise but I did & that's no thanks to you
that's all me.

Ibukunwrites

Mania

I awaken early in the morning when no else has stirred.

My fevered eyes darting wildly

No fever to speak of

Just an amazing undercurrent of electricity running throughout my body.

The sparkling light is so bright yet I welcome it with open arms.

I feel so powerful

I feel so perfect

Everything sparkles

Each of my senses is heightened

I feel strong

I feel magical

I don't need sleep

I feel superhuman

Oh my God I'm not sad

Oh my God I'm not sad

What a relief of being in the darkness

I feel better than normal

I feel surprisingly extra special wonderful

Why would anyone not want to feel this?

Everything is wonderful until…

Until the point where I feel out of control

Out of control anger

Out of control distrust

My fears show up in voices and hallucinations

So overwhelming I am beside myself

Then one day I am better

I feel normal

Only to fall yet again when I am triggered once again.

Daisy Bojorquez

O'brother

I thought I had a brother.
At least that's what everyone said
But it turns out to him I was already dead.
I thought i had a brother.
I told him my secrets and exposed my fears
But he just turned to me and said "you're a hoe and you're Queer"
I thought I had a bother.
For when I really needed help.
But he showed me that he could only do for himself.
I thought I had a brother.
I believed it inside
Till he threaten me in front of my family with that look in his eyes
I thought I had a brother.
But now I know the truth,
He seen me as weak and thought I was crazy too.
O'brother.

Vincent J Osborne

Rainbow

walking under the rainbow,
The rainbow of life,
Born into a shell layered nice and high,
Told who you are and why to confide,
Truly just hiding through the pride,
Trying to rely on Cesar to guide,
Trying not to cry,
Not ready to fully commit but you give it a try,
Thrown into adulthood with nothin but school,
one day you drop out and all hell breaks loose,
The curtains fall down, all is shown,
Too scared to seek the truth,
Half way through and your time has came,
Crashing down like nova cane,
In balm beach with some bikini,
Waving start to finish,
Waiting for me to end it,
But I see the treasure behind that pain,
So I floor it and ride through the rain.

Intellectual Difference

Even The Darkest Souls

Too many voices

Not enough ears

So many peers

Too many fears

Not enough love

So much hate

Too many tears

Not enough choices

So many days

Too many sores

Not enough care

So much rough

Too many fake

Not enough air

So many poisons

Too many faces

Not enough real

So much tainted

Too many places

Not enough saints

So many feelings

Pull this anxious soul out of me

Soak it in the riverbed of transcendence

rinse it well

rinse it clean

let clarity and my being blend

becoming one with the stream

current flowing over

serpents swimming under

allowing sustenance to mend

even the darkest souls

can bleed out the negativity

Sabrina Eden

Depression

Alogia and Catatonia

I can't form words

I am in my own space

My fight has gone grim

This life has swallowed me in malice

There's an equation to this madness

In which, others see as unresponsive

My sight has gone dark, a never ending tunnel

This world has immersed me in sadness

There's an invasion on my palace

In which, I see every toxin

My light has grown dim

As I walk

As I sit

As I stand

I feel unbalanced

Functioning is a challenge

Alogia and catatonia

My only companions

in my mass

of condensed density

Sabrina Eden

Anxiety

I can hear my heart racing
I can feel my palms itching
These thoughts I cannot stop thinking
I can tell its fear lurking in the corners of my heart
demons wrestling my resistance to explode
I am doing my best to hold them back
but I no longer can tell how long my mind-resistance
is going to work
it's becoming cold around me
my hands have goose pimples written all over them
I can feel my mouth shaking; my words shaky
my jaw and my teeth trying hard to stay calm
these anxiety music sucks.
but I've learnt to cater to days like this
days I need extra help in winning anxiety
so, I dip my hands in my bag
I bring my pills out
just one will do
this pill life is not an easy one
but every time we pop one to keep our rushing emotions
from snuffing life out of us
we're conquering warriors
choosing life when death beckons.

Ibukunwrites

Broken

Why did you do that to me?

You changed my life forever in the worst way.

I trusted you.

You made me feel safe.

You were my friend.

How could you break my trust?

You called me to your room and I went like a lamb to the slaughter.

Little did I know that action would change me forever.

How could you?

How could you?

After the nightmare my poor little body...

My poor little mind could not sustain the grief, the pain and the guilt of the world.

It all sunk down into the deepest recesses of my brain.

I couldn't handle it.

I didn't know how.

Fear griped me tightly every single day and every single night.

I never felt so alone...

How could you?

How could you?

Daisy Bojorquez

Cry

Please just let me cry.

I need to cry.

Please just let me cry.

A single raindrop has turned to an ocean of pain.

I feel the heaviness in my chest.

Emotions are not wrong.

Then why oh why do others think bad of it?

I'm drowning...

I'm drowning...

Stop telling me I'm ok.

I'm not ok.

You are telling me to just smile through the pain.

Just don't talk about it.

Just get over it.

So much unexpressed...

Oh God I'm drowning.

Daisy Bojorquez

Happiness

I hide it all within me because I do not know how to explain this turbulence in my soul.

All that I feel inside is too deep for tears.

I try to make myself believe I am so strong yet I feel so weak.

A single tear falls from my eye.

And my happiness just slips away...slips away...into the darkness...into oblivion.

I struggle on but not for myself.

It is only for those that I love.

My mind slips in and out of darkness...

I struggle to keep alive.

As I do what I must do I am leaving some behind...

they have given up and no longer want the struggle.

And my happiness just slips away...slips away...into the darkness...into oblivion.

I fight against this twisted world where everyone feels pain...a world I must escape.

My mind...my heart...struggles to free itself and for a moment I feel it...

Happiness...

I love them but then they just say goodbye.

I look into their eyes and fight the surge of pain and sorrow.

And my happiness just slips away...slips away.

Daisy Bojorquez

Here

Intimacy lead to the death of me,
slowly envisioning things right in front of me,
blinded by worldly things,
maybe when I clear my head,
I will be fixed again,
ready to give it a try but not ready to die trying,
wanting to fly away from all the hate I see on tv,
Hopefully to a place where I can finally rest my face.

Intellectual Difference

I Survived All by Myself

I survived all by myself
your words hurt me than it built me
your voice scared me into silence
than it taught me to find my words
so when I heard you took credit for my survival
I put it to you
my strength came from all of me & none of you
you didn't make me I made me
each time you knocked me down and I rose
I made me.

Ibukunwrites

Light in the Darkness

The star's lights are like holes in the curtain of night through which the angels peep at me.

The light teases my eyes.

The dense air traps my body in its prism.

Soft music floats to my ears keeping me awake.

While the smell of fragrant roses fills my nostrils, tickling them.

The night's darkness and the blue moon embrace me and kiss my skin and while the lights dance around my eyes I taste the darkness.

Dreams of moonlight and stars engulf me.

I step lightly on the clouds of my thoughts and bask in the ethereal glow of the bright crescent in the skies.

As I begin to wake my thoughts now turn to you...

I wonder how you are...if you slept well at night.

What did your dreams consist of my friend?

Where you happy in your sleep?

Did you find some peace...?

Though we are far apart there are times I can feel your nearness.

But then... I wake and find you are not there.

My eyes fill with unshed tears.

I miss you...

As the moon and the night engulf my being once again I fly inside my mind, sinking into the deepness, and thinking of sweet dreams that may or may not come true.

Daisy Bojorquez

Live Like A Love Song

I add to my collection of memories and fears

Leaving behind dreariness in the air

Will I ever see the sun?

Can my illness be tamed?

I've tried so hard

I know all my problems won't fade

But if I can find a reason to smile

I can find a reason to stay

In high hopes that someday

I will find everything I need

To fill up my hollow body

To let my soul touch freedom

For life only lasts so long

Death is inevitable

Dear life,

Please prove me wrong

That people like us can too

Live like a love song

Sabrina Eden

Loneliness

Hold tight,
it will come when you aren't paying attention, at night,
when your guard is down, that's when it comes out from the shadows,
appearing in your window,
ready to grab your soul,
taking it far from here,
burying it deep underneath,
somewhere only you can see,
with this thing this creature of greed travels from dream to dream,
ripping that out of the hands that need it to see,
themselves as wholesome things,
this creature destroys worlds, destroys dreams,
people who have almost nothing get that last thing taken with ease,
which makes them fiends to their own selfish dreams,
Loneliness is its name and murder and mischief is its game,
for it was once robbed of all his glory, thrown from heaven with no company,
swear to steal it from everybody,
swear to misplace that for our own selfish lust,
making us not different from the creatures crawling around us,
stay on the path of self love,
peace be with you and your company.

Intellectual Difference

Millions of Only

Is it just me or am I the only.

The only one who feels like this.

The only one to know this pain.

they call me crazy as if I'm the only one to go insane.

The only one to hate my life.

The only one to try to die.

The only one to run to truth.

The only one to hide my pride.

The only one to lie to doctors.

The only one to wear a mask.

The only one who lost my father.

The only one who acted rash.

The only one who got arrested.

The only one who tried to fight.

The only one they shouldn't mess with.

The only one who lost his life.

The only one who gave his all.

The only who learned to walk again,

When I couldn't even crawl.

I wondered if I were only or were there others like me?

The only way for me to know is to travel the world and see.

Vincent J Osborne

Panic Attacks

It's 2am
I am cold
my palms are sweaty
I can't breathe
tears running down my eyes
like water from a broken tap
my tear ducts are on fire
I can hear my heart fighting my chest
she wants out
I have no words
I cannot speak to her
my legs are shaking
my feet feel numb
I am not safe
I no longer want here
I just want this to stop
someone put me outta my misery
It's lonely here
someone please hold me
these moments take forever
It's chilly
I'm choking
someone
please
make this stop.

Ibukunwrites

Unique, Rest In Peace

Unique was her name

Only fifteen years old

Living in a world oh so cold

Who knows the horror of her extended home

She never told anyone

A decade has passed

I still wonder why

Beautiful, always smiling

Unique took her life

Alive, she could brighten anyone's day

All she's left behind is a lifetime of hurt

Wondering what we could have done to make her stay

Who's to say

Maybe it would have never been enough

Never let a beautiful smile

Or a contagious laugh fool you

She glowed on the outside

Decayed on the inside

For those who shine like the stars

Give off the most warmth

Unique was her name

But depression still took her life

nonetheless

Sabrina Eden

Space

Space the final frontier,
just another layer holding us here,
floating in the mind of our makers,
hope I get to witness the end,
before my time is cut lose, death welcome all,
that walk to its roots,
take the time to see the truth,
sprung out for the youth,
welcoming all willing to climb the tree of life,
making its presence alive,
before it flakes and dies,
before you finish these lines.

Intellectual Difference

Suicide

Sometimes, you discover you're at rock bottom
and there's no one holding you through.
Rock bottoms make us truly realize how alone we are;
that putting ourselves below and prioritizing others didn't get us nowhere.
So, when we find ourselves at rock bottom,
we are faced with two options – to do the uneasy;
pick ourselves up again for ourselves
or do the uneasy looking easy – walk away from (end) our own lives.

Ibukunwrites

The day I tried to die.

I couldn't stand the darkness

I felt suffocated

I knew this life wasn't for me.

Something told me self destruct. I'm giving in and I'm giving up.

Mom I think I've had enough.

My heart is full of bleeding cuts.

You all want more than I can be

I'm here for you not here for me. I know once I'm out there's no going back.

The doctors pulling me I hope my arms detach.

They got me out and now I'm blue.

There screaming and crying and I should be too.

They stab my neck so I can breathe

And I just want to go to sleep.

I'm here for them not here for me.

The day that I tried to die was

11/25/1989.

Vincent J Osborne

Tired

Enough

I've had enough.

I don't want to feel this way anymore.

I can't do this anymore.

I've felt this for too long.

Since I was too young I have felt sadness and despair.

My heart is so tired of this.

I know I need to keep living and breathing but

I'm so tired of being devastated each time my happiness slips away.

I don't want to be in the dark.

It hurts too much.

It makes it hurt to breathe.

I look into the faces of the ones I love through my tears.

Please I've had enough.

Daisy Bojorquez

Under Water

I keep gasping for air, I can't catch my breath.
My power is gone, my senses have left.
I feel my self-sinking, I wonder what can I do?
This loneliness I feel isn't anything new.
The more that I fight the deeper I sink.
Should I just open my mouth and gulp down the sea?
There's pain head and fear I'm my gut.
But they tell me keep quiet, don't speak of such.
I know I'm not crazy, but maybe I am
Would God give me a battle that I couldn't win?
The medication won't work and nobody cares.
I can't wait till the day I lay lifeless and bare.
As tough as it is i know I can win.
I just have to keep people from getting under my skin.
I lost my wife and maybe even my daughter.
So I ponder my death as I drift under water.

Vincent J Osborne

Uprooted

Done with these lies you throw,
done with the time holding me in place,
in the awkward second I'm your saving grace,
dumped when you find the prince,
I feel bruised and beaten, crushed beyond repair,
left to die in the cemetery,
aware of the pain you hide,
just to be the one princess he will find,
tucked away in a castle of your faith,
holding me locked away in the dungeon below,
depressing the feelings instead of showing them off.

Intellectual Difference

You

When it hurts to breathe, I make myself think of you.

No, you don't completely understand everything in my raging mind but you are still here.

You know my heart

You stay and love me unconditionally even though I feel I don't always deserve such happiness

I don't always feel that happiness

You have seen the ugliest forms of myself and you are still here

You know I always come back to my true self

Your love has saved me countless times

You accept my imperfection without hesitation

Your love is a perfect gift

I'm writing this down to be able to remind you of how much I truly love you

Daisy Bojorquez

Acceptance

An Open Letter For The Broken

You are not alone

in your millions of shattered pieces

We all lie amongst our floors

Begging to be swept away

Begging for the thickened clot to crease

To stop the flow

Of all the evil that has come our way

We have to gather ourselves

For another time

We must fall

to rise

It must rain

to see growth

Low and behold

We have to gather our valves

For another fight

We must stall

To receive a better taste of life

There are no handouts

That's not what life is about

We will find water in these droughts

Because that is what life is about

Overcoming

Evolving

Sacrifice is what it takes

Be relentless and you will find

Another way

Life's too short

To stay the same

So overcome the odds

Evolve relentlessly

This is what life is about

Fight with me

As I do, daily

Let glory be the end of you

Let glory be my legacy

Sabrina Eden

Bitter sweet

3 years gone.

I lived in a haze aloof to the throne

And when I came to it was the same old song.

The melody would change some sounded better.

Still I couldn't find the steps to this dance routine.

I had change my face and become better looking.

Lost weight and was eating healthy cooking.

The darkness was great but I didn't care.

3 years gone,

And he still wasn't there.

I realized the place I had come to first.

Turns out this empty soul was full of hurt.

Was my power gone? Or just out of touch.

3 years gone,

And I hadn't done much.

Therapist, psychologist, even naturopaths,

Couldn't prepare me for the aftermath.

I know that I can sit and wait but to me that would just be wasting another day

3 years gone,

In a medicated haze,

But the bitter sweet part is I have my clarity today.

Vincent J Osborne

Downstairs

Away from the danger above,

away from the aching pain overhead,

surrounded by the ones that take that feeling away,

safe and sound away from the truth, downstairs with you,

darkness surrounds me and I feel alone,

but I remember and look around to all the faces near,

Faces that also show fear,

so I feel more safe knowing others are lost too,

we are all in it together,

if you need a shoulder to cry on,

I will lend mine anytime,

just ask.

Intellectual Difference

Give Yourself A Free Range

sometimes, I swear
I want to be happy
but I'm too afraid to be
I tell myself
I'm not fine
so, it's not fair that I allow
myself be something else
other than sad.

Then I realize,
to withdraw permission from myself
to enjoy something else other than life-dictates
is unwholesome.
life is important and so am I.

so, to let yourself be happy is not
to betray your pain.
allow yourself to bloom
allow yourself to be
stop shutting the door on happiness
stop sabotaging what you deserve
stop placing your joy in handcuffs
uncuff. set it free.

Ibukunwrites

Hospital

Here I am again in a place meant to protect me from myself.

I already know the drill.

I wanted to be covered in the deep sleep of the dead a million times.

That's why I'm here right?

For protection of my dark wild thoughts?

I have to escape but my body holds me prisoner.

I know this is supposed to be a help.

A protection from yourself.

But why when all you want to do is pick up the shards of your life.

You want to try to piece them together despite your fear from pain that lies deep within.

Oh God what if you cut yourself with these shards.

You don't want to be stuck here.

You want to go back to your loved ones because you feel like a prisoner.

So just do what they want you to do.

Just smile.

Just keep on breathing even if it hurts.

Just keep your heart beating.

Even when you want the pain to end you know

deep down inside you do need your loved ones.

You need their support.

So I do what I'm supposed to do

So I just do what they want me to do.

Just smile.

Just keep on breathing even if it hurts.

Just keep my heart beating.

Daisy Bojorquez

I think she's right

I think it's something wrong with me.

I think she's more than I ever will be.

I think she made me crazy

I think I love hard

I think I had to grow old too soon

She just made it hurt more.

I think she's more than I ever will be.

I think she made me crazy

I think I love hard

I think I had to grow old too soon

She just made it hurt more.

I think she's more than I ever will be.

I think she made me crazy

I think I love hard

I think I had to grow old too soon

She just made it hurt more.

Vincent J Osborne

Ignorance

Not knowing is the hard part of existing,

but knowing isn't part of the journey,

but just as valuable as time and money, no time for mistakes,

use money to its fullest purpose,

know when to drop out of the rat race and acknowledge the beauty that surrounds you,

I'm done,

done with all the hate and peace that surrounds me,

done with this race and don't expect to find my place in this society of unconsciousness people, robots in disguise,

their only purpose is to put life to the side,

work for the play every second that comes by,

not caring about the things that catch their eye,

only worrying about next Friday,

when the paycheck comes in and you party it all away,

down the drain,

just like the generations before you,

just like the generations to come.

Intellectual Difference

I am a Warrior

I am a moving well of stories
A no-break wrestler of demons
and fallen angels
daily, I fight thoughts that
make attempts on my mind;
thoughts that try so hard to swap the truth
of the word with the truth of the world
I am a warrior
A walking
breathing
daily living miracle
and no,
I do not come to me by chance
No,
I do not give up my life without a fight!

Ibukunwrites.
In My Country

where I come from

silence is a communal heritage
we do not wash our dirty linens in public
mental illness is dirty
it's a dent
it's a shame
in my country
talking about things is not how we seek help
it's how we waste time
therapy is western
very alien to us
in my country
we don't feel
we pray
we don't listen
we give final and prescriptive opinions on people's illnesses
no, not illnesses
they are not ill
it's just life happening to them right?
it's not a big deal
depression is a feeling
something you snap out of
in my country
we do not understand how people can be rich and be depressed
depression is a broke man's fever
and a white man's disease.
in my country
we cheer people on when they publicize their suicidal notes
we read, snort
then we scream "go and die, say hello to Jesus for me"
in my country
mental health is a mockery
a ridicule, a comedy
something we don't try to understand
yet laugh at.
in my country everything is spiritual
we pick a bell
we torment the already tormented
he can hear voices
a soul is perishing
save a brother from hell
deliver him from the gates of hell
a fast, a break, a prayer session, a forced camping

let that demon lose, purge him of that alcohol addiction
he's seeing things
his village people must not win
pray him out of that bondage
pray for this brother again
deliver him from himself
I say, *"Deliver him from his brothers*
deliver him from his people,
set him free from religion,
get that man a therapy session."
They say to me, *"No, he needs a deliverance session*
this warfare is not carnal,
shall we pray? Olive (anointing) oil, holy water."

Ibukunwrites

In My Dreams

I wake in the middle of the night with a tear soaked face in his arms.

I was crying in my sleep again. That was the only way he knew to comfort my cries.

I don't always remember my dreams but I remember the emotions they invoked on to me as I slept. I felt the sadness. I felt the pain.

I think I even felt happiness for a brief moment.

A moment cut too short.

I wake up and it's not true.

I want it back.

I want it back.

Reality hits me hard in the face.

My dreams are so emotional I can hardly stand it.

Just let me dream that dream of happiness one more time.

Please just one more time.

Daisy Bojorquez

Living Schizoaffective

I get lost in things

that make me happy

I get lost in thoughts

that stab at me

I have to keep myself occupied

If I don't stay active

I imagine gory sights

Voices teasing

"You are not good enough

Imagine you dying"

"Everyone hates you

No sense in trying!"

I try so persistently to defy

The overactive

The tragic

Somedays, I want to give into my demons

But then I look at the reasons

To rebuild myself

I have family

I have goals

I have me

I am here to conquer,

every monster

that defends the status quo

Living schizoaffective is my greatest foe

Sabrina Eden

The Memories You Don't See (PTSD)

I am often misunderstood

Endless, explicit events

Out of every pattern I find

I know it's just in my mind

but I can't help but flinch

or twitch my eye

if only you could see what I hide

the innocence in the sway of a hand

Reminds me of an angry man

the innocence of a opened, clenched palm

Reminds me of another man's claws

the innocence of a date

Reminds me of the rape

the innocence of a man holding a pan

Reminds me of the boiling oil thrown on me, the memory of his laugh is rancid

the innocence of pulling out a chair

Reminds me of the one that I dodged, midair

the innocence of a tickle

Reminds me of my molester making me wiggle

I still feel the horrors of childhood

Leave me feeling broken and bent

I wish I could put my memories on display

When I am in a spell of dismay

So that I do not have to pretend that I am sane

Traumatic events have made me this way

Sabrina Eden

Peace Within

I cry out distressed and lamenting in a place where I have found comfort before...

I thought my peace would come easily as I watched the waves break along the shore...

walking barefoot... sensing it all...where is my peace...?

I find that there is sometimes a sorrow for which there is no relief...

I drift...

Twisting...

Turning...

I fall into the darkness of my inner being...

and then suddenly I am on the ground.

Broken and bleeding...

But still alive...

I close my eyes to dream and

I am swallowed by iridescent shades of blue and emerald green fire.

I swim in the ocean of blue lights and dance upon moonbeams.

I feel the slight caress of the gentle breeze upon my body and something within me stirs...

A feeling of intensity and depth.

I open my mouth and out pours my voice with songs of my past... my mourning song.

My body feels light now as I lay there engulfed by the new moon.

My eyelids flutter and then open...

the darkness is lighter...

I am in peace...

At least for a while...

Daisy Bojorquez

Royal Blood ; I Am Enough

There are things in this world
that have convinced me
Time & time again
That I am what others say
Once again I hover over this sink
digging these words out of my skin
Letting them spill into the drains
When people call us things,
Why do we take these sounds
And embed them into our brains?

I am not
You are not
Made up of sounds
Of another person
Or persons
In general
Yet here I am once again
Letting them hurt me
I am done being hurt by words
Of people who do not know my heart
Of people who can not read my mind

If only we could rinse off our scars
Tell them to goodbye
I guess we'll just have to find love

In so many things

That maybe

Just maybe

They'll become louder than the screams of those

who have us convinced that their words are more important

Than the paths we choose to lead

Watch me walk above the crowd

Of those whom are told that they are not

Good enough

Strong enough

Powerful enough

Wise enough

Follow the trail of blood

New words will fill my legacy

At the end of this trail

Everyone will notice my place

I will bleed from my throne

Because I chose to make it alone

Because we always have been

And always will be

enough

Act like it

And it will be so

Say it with me

"I Am Enough!"

Sabrina Eden

Spineless

Beauty redefines with time,

colliding colors with rhymes,

cramming dollars and dimes in the people's throat and eyes,

slowly crushing our bone and spines,

just a peak in our distant minds,

too blind to see the fine,

we paid way before we were made, to this world of hate,

each one of us specially made,

forgot with time,

way before we evolved the mind,

don't depress the feelings inside.

Intellectual Difference

Still here

Still here
still kicking it
sometimes, I'm tired
sometimes, I'm worn out
but I'm still here
and that's the only thing that matters;
that every day,
I refuse not to be.
Every day,
I fight for my life and defend my existence
every day,
I throw my fist in the air
I look at life from head to toe
and with my fears beneath my feet,
I stare death in the eyes
and I whisper to myself
"Today and again, you do not sink.
Baby girl, you float above these deepest waters
with your head up."

Ibukunwrites

Superhero

I never let the hate stick…

…Always let it bounce on the icy floor of reality…

I'm a hero in fact,

Showing the hate it has no place in my life to be intact,

Shattered the fake with one glance,

Destroyed the unfaithful with one laugh,

I am super cause I see that,

I am the one in control on my life and I will never look back,

let me live my life how I feel,

you can tell me I failed when I'm gone from here.

Intellectual Difference

Timeless

I might have to go that way with it.

I said don't play and she just kept kidding.

She didn't want me around and she didn't want to admit it.

I keep wasting time it just feels ridiculous.

I'll level up!

False evidence Appearing Real

I'll level up!

False Evidence Appearing Real

I'll level up!

False Evidence Appearing Real.

She killed me!

She didn't know I'd live on forever.

Vincent J Osborne

What People Say

I've heard it all before.

"Everyone goes through this."

"It's only a phase."

"She just turned 30. I went through this too. She will be fine. "

"It's all for attention."

All this does is minimize the fact that I need my loved ones.

The fact that I'm going through something real and at times horrifying.

Can't they see that even my own eyes tell the truth of what I'm going through?

Can't they see the tears in my eyes that tell my story?

Can't they see I'm actually jealous of those going through a simple phase?

These people get to leave this emotional turmoil behind.

I don't get to leave this behind.

It sometimes makes me feel angry.

The world can be very unfair.

I close my eyes to weep unshed tears.

I feel a heaviness in my chest whenever I breathe deeply to calm myself.

It's been so long since I cried because no one seems to understand.

I feel so alone.

I open my eyes and see and realize others suffering too.

Overwhelming feelings.

Overwhelming tears.

I am not alone.

You are not alone.

Daisy Bojorquez

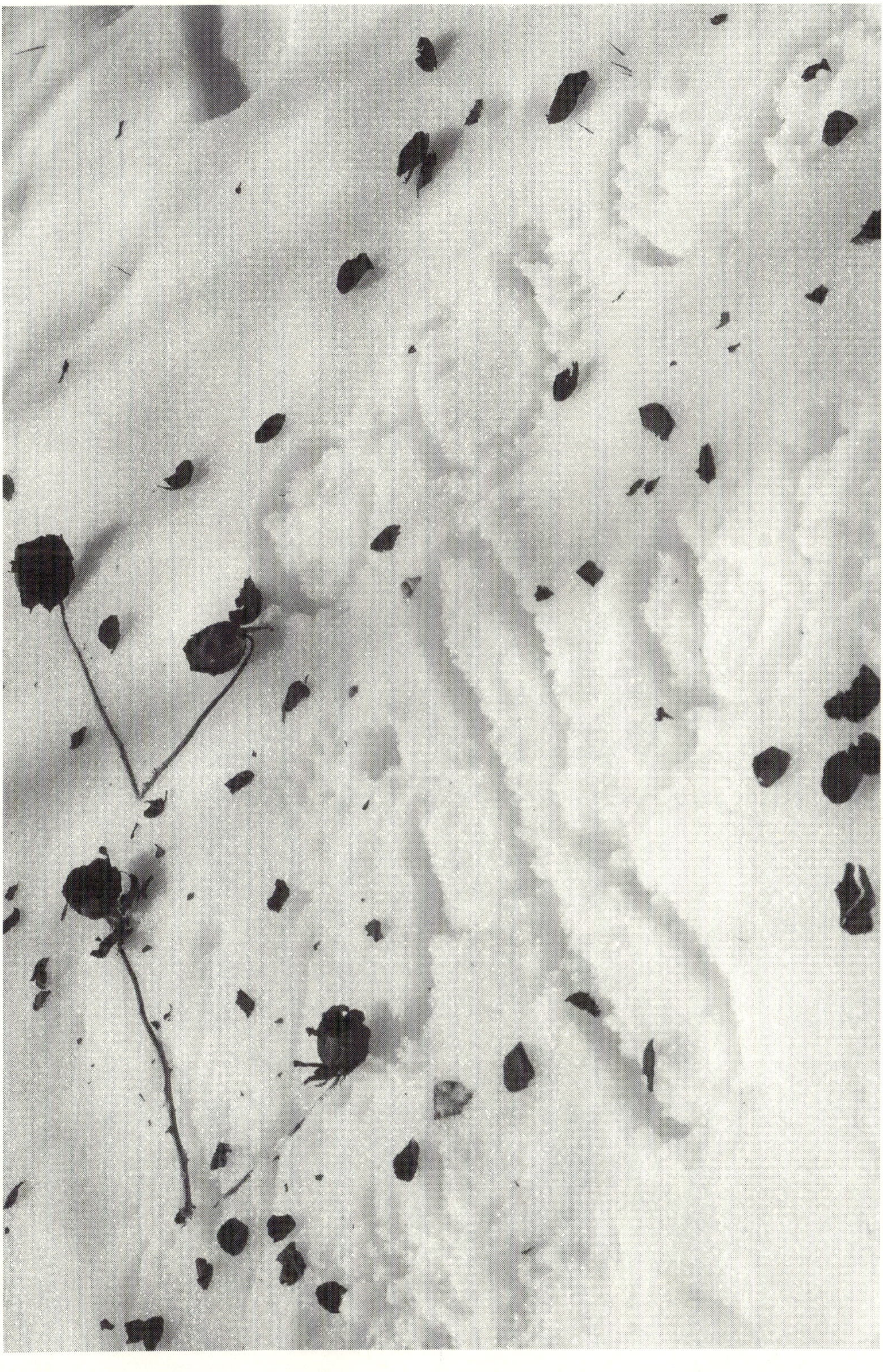

Appreciate

Breathe today

Because you can

Live today

Because someone else is on their deathbed

Yearning to be young again

Yearning to be freed from their pain

Breathe today

Because you have

A healthy beating heart

Live today

Because you have

Nothing standing your way

Nothing you can't take

For the dying's sake

Find your will to live

Breathe today

Because others do not get a choice

Live today

Because you have a voice

Defeat your bane

Reach out and find your campaign

I promise it will be okay

Things will change

Appreciate your life today

Sabrina Eden

Beautiful

The beautiful days are like gems shining from every facet in the sun.
Always remember the gems.
They will carry you in the deepest darkest days.
How far down does the deepness and the darkness go?
All the way down to the marrow of your bones.
You need the warmth of the sun of those precious days.
They will keep you alive for the day.
Remember them
Remember them.
You want to stay alive to see at least one more beautiful day.
One more embrace.
One more loving expression.
You need to stay alive to see at least one more beautiful day.

Daisy Bojorquez

Funmi

This is for Funmi
the woman who saw through me that broken vaginas
could make beautiful souls wrecked souls if help is withdrawn.
This is for Funmi
the woman who first saw beauty in my nakedness
before clothing me.
This is for Funmi
the woman who beheld first my purpose before
my eyes were ever open to see.
This is for Funmi
the woman who never stopped seeing the beauty in my heart
and the strength in me even in my most broken state.
This is for Funmi
the woman who confidently and fiercely demands my body from the waters
every time she tried to have it
This is for Funmilayo Mustapha
the reason my body always makes it back ashore with a pulse.

Ibukunwrites

Good morning sunshine on me

Good morning sunshine on me.
Good morning sunshine on me.
My happiness is eternal.
My soul is ablaze.
My tomorrow is promised.
Enjoy my today.
Good morning sunshine on me.
My happiness is eternal.
My soul is ablaze.
My tomorrow is promised.
Enjoy my today.
Good morning sunshine on me.
My happiness is eternal.
My soul is ablaze.
My tomorrow is promised.
Enjoy my today.

Vincent J Osborne

I refuse!

I won't concede.

I love the light within me.

I won't delete.

I love the breath that frees me.

They don't believe.

I know I can conquer anything because

I won't concede.

I love the light within me.

I won't delete.

I love the breath that frees me.

They don't believe.

I know I can conquer anything because

I won't concede.

I love the light within me.

I won't delete.

I love the breath that frees me.

They don't believe.

I know I can conquer anything because

I refuse to not Be!

Vincent J Osborne

Living Goals

To be fierce
to be bold
to own my thoughts in their most
unconventional & renegade states
to be recklessly devoted to art
& humanity
to love music with reckless abandon
to be vulnerable without love
& acceptance expectations
to be loved and to love in return
to dance and make rhythms
to be exceedingly joyful and fulfilled
to be kind to this body that has carried me
through so much
and at the end
this should be life as I lived it.

Ibukunwrites

On Getting Help

1. don't try to contain pain
   let it loose before you lose you.
2. don't wait for the boat to sink
   before you reach out for help;
   place an SOS while your head is still above water.
3. when you find yourself constantly slipping away
   and darkness is all you see
   draw the curtains and let the sun shine its light on and for you.
4. you're not weak because you live with a mental illness.
   you're not weak because you need pills to survive some worse days
   don't let people who have not looked fear in the eyes with their knees
   on the floor, birthing boldness repeatedly tell you it's insane refusing
   to go through life without help.
5. help doesn't have to be conventional.

Ibukunwrites

Prescription verbs

I wonder?

I wonder if they know?

I wonder if they know I know?

I wonder if they know I know how?

To Be.

I Am!

Made Wonderfully.

I wonder?

I wonder if they know?

I wonder if they know I know?

I wonder if they know I know how?

To Be.

I Am!

Made Wonderfully.

I wonder?

I wonder if they know?

I wonder if they know I know?

I wonder if they know I know how?

To Be.

I Am!

Made Wonderfully.

Vincent J Osborne

Reflection For Depression:

Alas!
We've seen the world's purest iris
These forms of apprehension
Can make even the dead squirm
The worms will stay nourished
But you,
Oh, the depressed
Are semi-realists
Alas!
Taking in life for what it really is
a vicious cycle
Waiting to begin
Dwelling in one side
Forgetting about the other
Reconcile!
In us there is hope
For one another
A kind of life you doubt
Unless you stick it out
Until you can figure what this life is about
Reconcile!
See the world through one another's pupils
Perhaps then we will all become one with the mutual
You see, chaos can not exist without harmony
If harmony were a mere constant
how could we tell the difference

between peace and conflict

Sabrina Eden

Self-care: This is how you keep breathing

On days when you find yourself walking outside hope
and into hopelessness,
remind yourself how far you've come
and drag yourself back into optimism.
on days when your heart become punctured holes
and you're broken by the people you love
and you stay feeling a little blue, unloved and loveless,
double wrap yourself in love and joy
and keep wrapping
daily wrapping
until you can say
I feel enough and I am enough by myself.
And
on days when death waits on you,
please, order life.

Ibukunwrites.

This is How You Fight the Hardest

On days when it feels so lonely
& you find yourself drifting off
& getting swamped with life
exhale the fear,
open your eyes,
breathe,
dare to fight and survive
trust yourself recklessly
and like never before
stretch yourself
look within and draw out
all of your strength
tell yourself,
this water is a making
and not a drowning
then push your head above water
and with an unfathomable confidence,
put one hand forward
and the other after
and like Khaleesi commands her dragons
you command your body *swim*.

Ibukunwrites

Unseen Beauty

Please oh please don't give up

I have felt your pain before

I feel it now

I feel the darkness trying to engulf me until I hear and see nothing

Blinded by my mixed emotions

Would they even care?

Would they be relieved once the burden is gone?

Would they even notice?

You might not believe the answer.

The answer is yes.

The darkness doesn't want you to believe.

It does want you to see the love you so completely deserve.

Please open your eyes.

Please open your heart.

I know it hurts.

But you need to see that there is beauty in this world.

You are valued.

You are special.

You are wanted and you are loved.

Please don't give up.

I care.

I care.

I beg you please don't give up.

Daisy Bojorquez

You're not alone

when life comes for you in sadness, pains
and despair,
remember you're not alone
when your mind hurts your bones
and your flesh becomes a haunted house
that you cannot wait to escape from,
hold on;
tightly to my hands through my words
and together, we'll recite hope to ourselves
saying
today,
we do not end our lives
so that fear can triumph.
today,
we do not breathe death
to give life to fear.

Ibukunwrites